Copyright

All rights reserved. No part of this workbook may be reproduced or transmitted in any form or by any means electronic or mechanical, including photocopying, recording, or by any information or retrieval system, without permission from the author, except for the inclusion of brief quotations in a review.

© Copyright 2013 by David Denniston. All rights reserved. 1st edition 2013.

Published in the United States of America.

About the Author

Dave Denniston, CFA is a financial advisor and author specializing working with physicians of all ages and enjoys particularly focusing on residents, fellows, and young physicians.

For years, he has seen slick salesman and insurance brokers giving poor advice that primarily benefits one person- the salesman.

He feels that it is time to enlighten and educate you on the ins-and-outs of insurance and how to minimize your costs rather than have them grow out of control.

His drive to help doctors came from the birth of his youngest child, Evangeline. She is his family's little miracle baby born in May 2012 four months prematurely at a weight of 12.5 oz (3.5 oz short of 1 pound!). As they were in the NICU for nearly five months, he had the opportunity to get to know many residents and fellows and listened to what they went through. He decided from then on that he was on a mission to help out any resident or fellow for free and the best way to do that was to write, speak, and meet with people individually to counsel them on their financial situation.

He is an expert in a number of financial planning topics including debt reduction, 457 DCs, 403bs, and other retirement plans, asset allocation (where to invest), disability income insurance, life insurance, annuities, college planning, stock awards and options, and much more.

He has written other workbooks on a variety of subjects that are available for sale on Amazon.com including- 45 *Secrets to Financing a College Education* and *5 Steps to Get Out of Debt for Physicians.* He is planning to write other workbooks on other subjects related to physicians on insurance planning, investments, and more.

He resides in Bloomington, MN with his wife of more than a decade, Cyrena, and his two children, Gabby and Evangeline.

For regular videos updates and newsletters on a variety of financial subjects, check out his website at www.daviddenniston.com/young-physicians or e-mail him at ddenniston@machtig.net.

Summary

Perhaps you are a young physician having just come out of medical school. No more tests or studying, you've just landed your feet!

Or maybe you are now in your residency or your fellowship and making a little bit of dough. You're starting to think about the future.

You are getting hit up by salesperson after salesperson who wants to sell you all kinds of financial advice- particularly on insurance. Maybe you've received a seminar invitation or two (or three or four or five)?

Why? Because you probably have not saved up much yet and insurance is a quick way for a smart salesman to make money today.

However, all of that being said, insurance is necessary for many reasons, particular for high-earning doctors with their whole career ahead of them and often a lot of debt behind them. Consider the following questions…

How would your family manage without your income if you died or become disabled?

How much do you have in reserves for the "stuff happens" in life events?

The bottom line- insurance, while necessary to protect our families, is a cost that should be minimized.

Explore and learn with me how you can minimize those insurance costs while having an appropriate amount of insurance for your specific situation. Take the next step- complete this workbook. Use this tool to reflect, strategize, and project yourself in the future. Revisit it on an annual basis.

If you would like any additional support and to learn more about how I can serve you, please feel free to contact me anytime at ddenniston@machtig.net or call me at (800) 548-1890.

Let's take this journey together and get you on the path to financial freedom.

Warm Regards,

Dave Denniston

Insurance Guide for Doctors Workbook

OVERVIEW | Not Another Plug for Any Insurance Company

First of all, this is not another plug for any insurance company. I am an independent financial advisor and wealth manager. I am not affiliated with any insurance company and I am doing this to help educate you and your family on how to navigate the confusing number of choices that you have available to you.

Regardless of who you work with, make sure that you are working with someone who gives you a multitude of choices and educates you on the cheapest option as well as the most expensive option. They should empower you with the information necessary to make an educated decision of either life insurance or disability income insurance.

Frankly, insurance of all types are over-sold in my opinion. My basic philosophy is when you are most vulnerable is when you need insurance the most. I encourage you to save and save and save so that you don't need an insurance company anymore and can be "self-insured" down the road.

Ultimately, my job is all about helping you making smart choices about your money and I believe this workbook will be a standard to measure others against as you speak with insurance consultants.

In this workbook, we are going to address the following:

- Disability Income Insurance- Overview. Group versus Individual Benefits
- Disability Income Insurance- Managing Costs Plus The Bells & Whistles (Riders)
- Disability Income Insurance- How to Compare One Company versus Another
- Life Insurance- Overview. How much should I have?

Insurance Guide for Doctors Workbook

- ➢ Life Insurance- Term versus Cash Value
- ➢ What Am I Spending Monthly & Where can I improve?

The exercises in this module are incredibly important in determining finding the right insurance for you. For many of us, this can be difficult to look at. Sometimes, we need a guiding hand.

<u>Don't hesitate to ask for help if you find you are procrastinating or just can't stand looking at the data on your own.</u>

MODULE One | Disability Income Insurance Overview

First, let's understand disability income (DI) insurance.

Why would you want DI insurance?

According to the Council of Disability Awareness and the Social Security Administration, illnesses like cancer, heart attack, diabetes, back pain, injuries, and arthritis are common causes of both long-term and short term disabilities. Further, almost three in 10 of today's 20 year-olds will become disabled before reaching age 67. That's 30 percent!

Additionally, the American Journal of Medicine (Vol 122, No 8) states that every 90 seconds someone files for bankruptcy in the wake of a serious illness.

This is a very real and present problem. According to the Standard Insurance Company, when disabilities do set it, the average duration below age 50 is five to six years.

How would your financial situation change if you weren't able to perform at your current capacity for five or six years? Voila! Disability Income (DI) insurance was created to protect against this risk.

There are two basic types- group DI and individual DI.

Group DI insurance is an employer-provided benefit. This may cost you little to nothing. Typically, the employer is using their own pre-tax dollars to provide a benefit to you, the employee. They are utilizing the law of large numbers to minimize the cost. Using the age of employees, compensation, claims history, and other information, the insurance company will work with the employer to determine the cost of benefit for all employees.

Note that because the benefits were funded with pre-tax dollars (by the employer usually) that the future benefit will be taxable income to you.

As long as you are using a certain level of benefit within the group, you don't have to go through any individual underwriting. This means that they don't look at your height, weight, or medical history. They won't take a blood draw or other bodily measurements.

For someone in generally poor health, above average build, or a negative medical history, maximizing your group insurance is a wonderful way to get insurance when you could not normally get it on your own.

Whereas, individual DI insurance will have the insurance company measuring all of these different criteria to determine whether you are healthy enough for the insurance company to offer you a policy or possibly add on some exclusions for particular existing health conditions.

Compared to group DI, you are using (unless self-employed) after-tax dollars in your own personal bank account. Note that because the benefits were funded with after-tax dollars (by you rather than the employer) that the future benefit will NOT be taxed.

Besides, the tax advantage, the major benefit of individual DI is that you have the control to customize a policy specifically for your needs.

For example…

Would you like your policy benefit to last until age 65 or just 5 years? It's your choice!

Would you like your policy to have a waiting period of 90 days or 180 days? It's your choice!

Would you like to have the ability to increase (or decrease) your coverage? You can do it.

Would you like to cover a small part, a medium-sized part, or a large part of your income? It's up to you!

We'll discuss in more detail the cost in dollars for each of these components (as well as others) as well as the differences between the "Big 6" insurance companies.

There are 6 traditional companies (the "Big 6") that insurance brokerage companies typically consider for physicians:

Standard, Principal, MetLife, Union Central (First Ameritas), Berkshire (Guardian), and MassMutual.

This is because each of these have included (or have an additional rider) a benefit of "Your Occupation" or "Own Occupation". We'll discuss this in more detail later.

Here are some general guiding thoughts that I would like to you consider:

- First, how dependent is your family on your income? Are you the sole bread-winner or a two family income? If a two family income, could your spouse's income cover living expenses and meet your debt obligations? The more dependent on your income, the more you will need disability income.

- While you have a substantial student debt load/mortgage, you should strongly consider having an individual DI policy. *Note that new rules released by the U.S. Department of Education could affect many Social Security beneficiaries who have student loan debt. Effective July of 2013, the repayment obligations of student loan borrowers who are deemed permanently and totally disabled by Social Security may be discharged.* They key here is "permanent" and you have to have approval from the Social Security Office. If you are partially disabled or for a period that is not "permanent", you will still owe regular payments on your student debt.

- The longer the period until retirement, you have a larger potential income and savings you have to lose. After you have been out of residency/fellowship for 10 to 15 years, you should hopefully be close to "self-insured" and the need for career-long disability insurance should drop. At that point, consider a cheaper individual policy (i.e. lower benefit or lower time period) or just stick with the group term benefit.

- Make sure besides 401k/tax deferred savings vehicles that you are consistently saving in a non-qualified account (not subject to early withdrawal penalties, like a bank account or "regular" investment account), to protect against the "rainy day" conditions like a disability. Once you have $150k or more (in today's dollars) in a combination of the 401k and non-qualified accounts, I would consider you at least partially "self-insured" assuming your annual living expenses are $60k (in today's dollars) or less. The more in non-qualified, in particular, the better. Although, in most cases you can take a tax-free loan in a 401k up to 50% of the value or $50,000 whichever is less as long as you pay it back over a handful of years.

- Make sure to have the agent helping you get quotes from three different insurance companies and explain the differences between them. Don't be shy to ask how much business the agent does with each of these companies and how they decide between them.

Insurance Guide for Doctors Workbook

Below is a summary chart that is NOT comprehensive, but explains the basics of comparing and contrasting a typical group DI policy versus an individual policy:

Typical Group Policy	Typical "Big 6" Individual Policy
Little to no medical underwriting required. Neither age or health will usually matter At time of application.	Substantial medical and financial Underwriting required. Better the younger & Healthier you are.
Cheapest Option	Usually more expensive, depending upon the riders you select
If paying for the policy, get a tax deduction. If benefits are paid, they are taxable.	Benefits are tax-free (assuming paid From post-tax account)
Premiums paid monthly at no extra cost	Premiums best paid annually. Quarterly or Monthly costs more.
After 24 months, any new income-producing job" i.e. "NOT Own Occupation" will subtract from benefit	Comes with or can add rider for "Own Occupation". This means that you can Work anywhere after being disabled and can Maintain DI benefit plus new earned income
Contract terms, premiums, and benefits can Change at any time	Comes with or you add a rider for "non-cancellable & guaranteed" to ensure that premiums and benefits cannot change
Policy ends when you end employment	Policy is carried by you, before and after employment with any employer
No partial-disability benefit	Has a partial disability benefit (15 to 20% or more loss of income minimum)

For more information, go to www.daviddenniston.com/physicians.
For questions, e-mail: ddenniston@machtig.net
Or call 800-548-1820

1.1 Action Step: Gather together information on your current group disability income policy and fill in the information below:

Current Benefit Amount:_____

What is the maximum benefit:_____

How long does it cover "own occupation":_____

How much does it cost me:_____

Does it include partial disability?_____

How (if any) does it rise with inflation:_____

1.2 Action Step: Consider your current financial situation. How much debt (consumer, student, home) do you have? How much in liquid accounts (bank, investments) do you have? Do you have enough for 5 to 10 years of living and liability expenses?

Would your current group term DI cover those needs? For how long?

Are you a sole breadwinner or does your family have two incomes?

Write your thoughts down below on the need for individual DI for your situation.

_____

_____

_____

_____

Insurance Guide for Doctors Workbook

MODULE Two | Managing Costs Plus Bells & Whistles

Now that we've covered the basics of DI policies and why they are necessary, let's explore the costs for given benefit levels.

First, depending upon your specialty and area of practice, the costs can vary. The insurance companies can deem one specialty as "less risky" than another.

The "less risky" specialties are cheaper! According to the Disability Insurance website, a common insurance carrier had 5 different rankings (least to highest risk): Class 4m, Class 3m, Class 2m, Class 1m, and Not Eligible. Below is a table of how common medical occupation specialties are classified:

Class 4m		Class 3m	
Audiologists	Neurologists (no surgery)	Anesthesiologists	Mid-Wives
Cardiologists	Internist	Dentists	Nurse Anethetist
Dermatologists	Opthalmologists	ER Physicians	Podiatrists
Family Practice	Pathologists	Medical Assistants	Surgeons (all specialties)
General Practice	Psychiatrists	Medical Technicians	X-Ray Technicians
Genetic Physicians	Radiologists		
Hospital Admin.	Urologists		

Insurance Guide for Doctors Workbook

Let's introduce several terms that determine the cost of the policy:

1) Monthly Benefit- the monthly paycheck you would receive from an insurance company in lieu of your disability (assuming total disability or a percentage for a partial disability). The higher the benefit, the higher the cost. The lower the benefit, the lower the cost.

2) Benefit Period- the maximum length that your benefit can last. This could be 2 years, 5 years, 10 years, to age 65, or to age 67. The longer the period, the higher the cost. The shorter the period, the lower the cost.

3) Waiting Period- the amount of time from claim accepted to the time your monthly benefit starts. This is a little different- the longer the insurance company doesn't have to pay your claim, the bigger the discount they will give you. The longer the period, the lower the cost. The shorter the period, the higher the cost.

What should you ask an agent for?

I generally suggest to ask for a couple of different monthly benefits levels (40%, 50%, 60% if in practice, 40k, 50k, 60k if a resident/fellow) as well as a couple of different benefit periods.

The cheapest possible individual policy you could have is an extremely low monthly benefit (i.e. $1,000/mo), a 2 year benefit period, and a 365 day waiting period.

Whereas, the most expensive individual policy you could have is an extremely high monthly benefit (think 80% of your practicing compensation), to age 67 benefit period, and a 60 day waiting period.

I suggest for most residents, fellows, and young practicing physicians who have lots of student debt and very little in assets- a medium monthly benefit (40% to 60% of practicing income), benefits to age 65, and a 90 day waiting period is fairly reasonable.

As we mentioned earlier, the more you become self-insured the less of a benefit you need. Let's say your student debt is now paid off and you have built up a portfolio of $200,000 (in today's dollars). It's worth taking a look at your current policy and changing the benefits accordingly by lowering the monthly benefit, decreasing the benefit period, and increasing the waiting period. You don't need as much insurance now! Why pay for something you don't need?

For more information, go to www.daviddenniston.com/physicians.
For questions, e-mail: ddenniston@machtig.net
Or call 800-548-1820

Insurance Guide for Doctors Workbook

Let's explore a few examples:

Below is a table taken from an illustration for the Standard for an Anesthesiologist, **age 26**, at $3,000/month benefit. The costs listed below are annual premiums.

Benefit Period	Waiting Period			
	60 Days	90 Days	180 Days	365 Days
2 Years	$1,054.10	$785.90	$716.18	$627.87
5 Years	$1,244.51	$936.04	$854.72	$749.82
10 Years	$1,524.10	$1,143.91	$1,045.36	$916.99
To Age 65	$2,143.71	$1,597.76	$1,459.72	$1,281.74
To Age 67	$2,260.27	$1,683.65	$1,538.61	$1,350.26

Below is a table taken from an illustration for the Standard for an Anesthesiologist, **age 26**, at $3,750/month benefit. The costs listed below are annual premiums.

Benefit Period	Waiting Period			
	60 Days	90 Days	180 Days	365 Days
2 Years	$1,234.25	$915.12	$834.61	$732.80
5 Years	$1,445.97	$1,079.14	$985.67	$865.85
10 Years	$1,774.23	$1,322.19	$1,208.34	$1,061.22
To Age 65	$2,511.59	$1,861.76	$1,701.15	$1,495.19
To Age 67	$2,649.60	$1,963.17	$1,794.21	$1,576.24

Below is a table taken from an illustration for Principal for an Anesthesiologist, **age 26**, at $3,750/month benefit. The costs listed below are annual premiums.

Benefit Period/ Your Occupation Period	Disability Base Elimination Periods (In Days)				
	30	60	90	180	365
To Age 70/To Age 70	$3,728.72	$2,200.52	$1,803.29	$1,680.09	$1,571.76
To Age 67/To Age 67	$3,654.80	$2,126.94	$1,730.04	$1,606.86	$1,498.52
To Age 65/To Age 65	$3,600.80	$2,072.27	$1,675.36	$1,552.84	$1,444.17
5 Year/5 Year	$2,323.48	$1,209.48	$893.49	$815.11	$731.76
2 Year/2 Year	$1,994.65	$966.15	$653.72	$534.02	N/A

For more information, go to www.daviddenniston.com/physicians.
For questions, e-mail: ddenniston@machtig.net
Or call 800-548-1820

Insurance Guide for Doctors Workbook

Below is a table taken from an illustration for Principal for an Anesthesiologist, **age 29**, at $3,750/month benefit. The costs listed below are annual premiums.

Benefit Period/ Your Occupation Period	Disability Base Elimination Periods (In Days)				
	30	60	90	180	365
To Age 70/To Age 70	$4,144.18	$2,637.23	$2,162.38	$1,990.25	$1,855.25
To Age 67/To Age 67	$4,048.33	$2,542.40	$2,066.87	$1,895.76	$1,760.09
To Age 65/To Age 65	$3,977.45	$2,471.19	$1,995.98	$1,824.54	$1,688.87
5 Year/5 Year	$2,534.01	$1,437.84	$1,052.37	$951.21	$852.16
2 Year/2 Year	$2,125.75	$1,133.95	$755.25	$613.47	N/A

Below is a table taken from an illustration for Principal for an Anesthesiologist, **age 26**, at $5,000/month benefit. The costs listed below are annual premiums.

Benefit Period/ Your Occupation Period	Disability Base Elimination Periods (In Days)				
	30	60	90	180	365
To Age 70/To Age 70	$4,740.50	$2,817.00	$2,313.50	$2,154.50	$2,015.50
To Age 67/To Age 67	$4,646.50	$2,723.00	$2,220.00	$2,061.00	$1,922.00
To Age 65/To Age 65	$4,576.50	$2,652.50	$2,149.50	$1,991.50	$1,852.00
5 Year/5 Year	$3,261.00	$1,697.50	$1,254.00	$1,144.00	$1,027.00
2 Year/2 Year	$2,799.50	$1,356.00	$917.50	$749.50	N/A

Let's review over some of these differences.

First, I have used these illustrations as snapshots in time. The insurance companies can change their rates at any time and these may or may not reflect your situation which is dependent on your specialty, age, health, etc.

We can see from each of these illustrations that there are substantial differences in premium if you move to the extremes.

For example, if you use a 90 day elimination period and a benefit period to age 65 for the $5,000 illustration above, you are right in the middle at $2,150/year.

If you cut the elimination period to 30 days, you more than double the cost at about $4,600/year!

For more information, go to www.daviddenniston.com/physicians.
For questions, e-mail: ddenniston@machtig.net
Or call 800-548-1820

Whereas if you cut the benefit to being only 2 years, you cut the cost more than one-half to about $900/year!

Note that there is some difference in premium between benefit periods to age 65 and age 70, or between 90 days and 180 days elimination periods.

However, the dramatic difference occurs when you cut the benefit to 5 years or less or when you increase the elimination period from 30 days to 60 days at Principal (or 60 days to 90 days at the Standard).

Additionally, there is a dramatic difference in premium when you wait to get disability income. Using the $3,750 monthly benefit, 90 day elimination period, benefit to age 65…

At age 26, the cost is $1,675.35/year whereas at age 29, the cost jumps up dramatically by almost 20% to $1,995.98/year.

In this example, if you decide to get the DI insurance as a resident, you are giving up the use of 3 years of premiums ($5,026.05) in order to avoid a higher annual cost ($320.63/year).

This is about a 15 year break-even. If you hold this DI policy past age 41 (assuming you bought at age 26), you will have made the best possible financial decision.

I think either is a fine decision, the main point is to have the protection in place.

However, keep in mind that you want to lock in your rates while you are a resident or fellow.

Most of the "big 6" insurance companies will allow you to underwrite up to a $5,000/month benefit or $6,000/month benefit before you get into practice. This will make sure that you are getting close to 40% to 60% of your income coverage between your individual DI and group DI.

Once you are in practice, the insurance companies typically restrict how much they will underwrite in coordinating with your group policy, which is far more limited in benefits and your ability to use it.

Next, let's review over the bells & whistles (riders) that you can add onto your disability income policy.

Here are the riders that I suggest to strongly consider:

- Own Occupation/Regular Occupation
- Residual Disability & Recovery Benefit
- Guaranteed Insurability/Future Purchase Option

- Guaranteed Renewable and Noncancellable
- Cost of Living Adjustment (COLA)

Own Occupation/Regular Occupation – For physicians, this is a particularly important rider.

Imagine what would happen if you had to quit your job due to a disability. Maybe you developed arthritis or a horrible pain in your neck forced you to call it quits as a physician or perhaps limit your hours.

Yet, you want work in another occupation because the disability income is not enough to maintain your standard of living (as well as to do something useful with yourself!). After all, you are used to making $200,000 to $400,000 per year. How many other jobs could replicate that kind of income?

Without this rider, you could not get a claim from your disability policy.

This rider ensures that if you are no longer able to operate and do procedures as a physician that you could receive income from <u>another occupation</u> (i.e. teaching at a University or becoming a financial advisor) in addition to your disability income insurance check.

Specifically, "Specialty Occupation/Own Occupation/Regular Occupation" covers a "job that you are suitably trained and qualified for".

<u>Some of the "Big 6" differentiate between speciality occ and own occ (or regular occ).</u> Truly, specialty occupation does have a more specific definition related to being a physician. However, several brokerage companies I have spoken with have thought that this is merely a marketing gimmick that allows the insurance company to charge higher rates for the rider.

If you feel strongly, more comfortable, and have better peace of mind with one or the other, that's great. Keep in mind that I'm trying to help you keep down your costs.

Either would work fine, the point is to make sure to include it!

Residual Disability & Recovery Benefit -

This is the official name of the rider. I prefer to call it "partial" disability.

As noted in the table comparing group DI versus individual DI, most group policies do not cover partial disability.

This rider ensures that if you can still work as a physician, but you need to work less than usual due to a disability- a minimum of 30% up to 80% is typical- for a period longer than your elimination period then you can receive a check from your disability policy.

If this rider is not included, then partial disability will not be covered.

Ironically, partial disability for less than five years is the most common occurrence of disabilities. I am sure this is due to the "stuff happens" in life- the skiing accident that caused you to break a leg or perhaps the years of bending over and overstretching your neck. My dentist recently had to take a fully disability and get away from his practice due to the latter issue.

Guaranteed Insurability/ Future Purchase Option -

Many physicians start out with a significantly lower income than what they end up having a few years down the road.

Perhaps, they become a partner in the practice or they are promoted to a leadership position. Also, perhaps they are in a grace period for the first year or two while their clinic tests their mettle and sees what they are made of.

Whatever the case, the difference in income can be substantial two years or more out of practice. While the young physician is paying back their student debt and starting to accumulate their assets, they may not be in a strong enough financial position to lower their disability income- they may want to even increase it.

This rider ensures that they can purchase more insurance for specific increments at a given point down the road (1 years, 2 years, or 3 years depending upon the company) without going through underwriting again. Your health will not be considered.

Note that some companies like Principal will give you the opportunity at a specified time (3 years in their case) to purchase additional disability income insurance without underwriting. If you choose not to increase your insurance, the future purchase option will cease to exist.

Alternatively, if you think your income may be capped out and has limited ability to increase OR you could maintain your desired standard of living within the limits of your disability policy, don't include this rider!

Guaranteed Renewable and Non-cancellable – These are two separate terms that can be automatically included with your contract or added on as separate riders.

Make sure that you understand the difference between the two as well as whether or not they are automatically included.

If you do not have these riders, the insurance company could cancel your policy (along with others in the same age/type category) and raise the premium at will.

To illustrate an example, let's review over the difference between Principal and The Standard.

I recently ran a quote for a client where Principal and Standard came up as the best two options. Both included provisions for guaranteed renewable and/or non-cancellable.

The Principal contract was slightly more expensive and is BOTH non-cancellable and guaranteed renewable whereas The Standard contract is slightly cheaper and is ONLY guaranteed renewable.

The difference between the two is non-cancelable which means Principal cannot change or cancel your policy, except for nonpayment of premiums, or increase the premiums before you reach age 65, regardless of changes in your income, occupation or health.

In comparison, Standard could not cancel the policy (except for unpaid premiums), but could raise the premiums for all people in your age and occupation class.

To quickly sum up, The Standard's contract in this example was cheaper but premiums could potentially rise in the future whereas Principal's contract had a locked in price even thought it was slightly more expensive.

Either are fine contracts, just be aware of the choices!

COLA (Cost of Living Adjustment) -

Every year the cost of stamps, milk, and gas seem to go up automatically. Many folks refer to this effect as inflation.

As a financial advisor, I counsel people constantly to make sure to plan for rising costs while they are working or in retirement.

If you think you might need to plan for future living expense increases, this is the purpose of a COLA rider. This way your disability income in the future could keep up with inflation.

This is a worthwhile rider to consider.

Insurance Guide for Doctors Workbook

Here are the riders that I would strongly suggest to avoid in order to minimize costs. I am not going to describe them in the detail I have above, but if you have any questions as to the why, please let me know:

- Catastrophic Disability
- Social Security Rider
- Hospital Income Rider
- Lifetime extension rider
- Waiver-of-premium rider
- Accidental death & dismemberment rider
- Return of premium rider

2.1 Action Step: Get quotes from two different companies for your income level at 40% of your current compensation (or 40k if a resident/fellow). Fill in the table below.

Elimination Period/ Benefit Period	60	90	180	365
2 Years				
5 Years				
To Age 65				
To Age 67				
To Age 70				

2.2 Action Step: Get quotes from two different companies for your income level at 50% of your current compensation (or 50k if a resident/fellow). Fill in the table below.

Elimination Period/ Benefit Period	60	90	180	365

Insurance Guide for Doctors Workbook

2 Years				
5 Years				
To Age 65				
To Age 67				
To Age 70				

2.3 Action Step: Get quotes from two different companies for your income level at 60% of your current compensation (or 60k if resident/fellow). Fill in the table below.

Elimination Period/ Benefit Period	60	90	180	365
2 Years				
5 Years				
To Age 65				
To Age 67				
To Age 70				

Now that you have defined your different possibilities, take some time to reflect on the best choice.

2.4 Action Step: What is the amount of protection you need for the future- 40%/50%/60% (or 40k/50k/60k if resident/fellow)?

If you have a relatively low amount of assets relative to your income, consider a lower elimination period, 90 days at the most.

How long do you want to protect your income? Consider at least 5 years if you have less than 5 years of your living expenses saved up. Which of these scenarios best fit your budget?

Write your thoughts down below.

Insurance Guide for Doctors Workbook

_____
_____
_____
_____
_____

2.5 Action Step: Review over the optional riders from earlier in the text- Specialty Occupation/Own Occupation/Regular Occupation, Residual Disability & Recovery Benefit, Guaranteed Insurability/Future Purchase Option, Guaranteed Renewable and Noncancellable, and Cost of Living Adjustment (COLA)

Which of these could best fit your situation?

Write your thoughts down below.

_____
_____
_____
_____

MODULE Three | How To Compare DI Companies

Now that we have quotes from two different companies. How can you compare and contrast between them? What are the differences between the companies and the quotes?

As a licensed agent, one of the more frustrating aspects is understanding what the difference between company A and B. Why should a client go with company A over company B?

Is the lowest premium the right solution? Does company B offer something significantly different from company A?

This is the best information that I could collect on the differences between the "big six" carriers through mid-2013 and could change on a moment's notice. I will work to update this list on an annual basis.

Basic Contract Features, Exclusions, & Special Features

	Ameritas	Berkshire/ Guardian	Mass Mutual	MetLife	Principal	Standard
Contract Type	Non-cancel Able & Guar Anteed Renewable	Non-cancel Able & Guar Anteed Renewable	Non-cancel Able & Guar Anteed Renewable	Non-cancel Able & Guar Anteed Renewable	Non-cancel Able & Guar Anteed Renewable	Non-cancel Able & Guar Anteed Renewable
Mental & Nervous Disability Exempted	24 month Limitation	Unlimited	24 month Limitation	Unlimited	24 month Limitation	Unlimited
Special Features	Nondisabling Injury, COBRA Premium, Survivor Benefit, Good Health, Transplant Surgery, Cosmetic Surgery, Social Insurance Substitute	Capital Sum, Transplant Surgery, Waiver of Elimination Period	Dividends, Long Term Care Purchase Credits	Transplant Surgery, Suspension During Unemployment	Capital Sum Benefit, Supplement Health Bene, Transplant Surgery Benefit, Accidental Death	Compassionate Care, Survivor Benefit

For more information, go to www.daviddenniston.com/physicians.
For questions, e-mail: ddenniston@machtig.net
Or call 800-548-1820

Diffe r en

Within a basic disability policy, there can be some differences. As noted in the previous table, mental & nervous disorders can have a 24 month exclusion in many policies. How concerned are you not only with physical health, but also your mental health? How subject have you and blood relatives been to mental disorders or substance abuse? If there have been past history with these issues, it will make sense to use a company without any limitations.

While I listed many additional benefits, I do not think that these should be taken into consideration. I like to think of them as additional "bonuses". You have them for no additional cost and they aren't worth paying extra for separately.

Differences Between Riders

One of the biggest differences between carriers lies in the legal language.

A primary example of this is the definition of total disability. This is directly related to the rider for own occupation. There can be a difference between *"own occupation" or "specialty occupation"*.

For the most part, the legalese is fairly repetitive between the carriers, but by adding additional language, some folks may feel more protected from a conservative insurance company.

Some are brief and to the point while others are longer and more descriptive.

I would point to a couple of carriers as primary examples.

Principal has the shortest definition, "Means solely due to Injury or Sickness *you are unable to perform the substantial and material duties of Your Occupation* and should you choose to work in another occupation, you'll receive full benefits, regardless of the income you earn from the other occupation."

In comparison, Ameritas has a fairly length definition. "Means that due to a sickness or injury, in and of itself, *you are not able to perform the material and substantial duties of your occupation and you are not working in any occupation for wage or profit*. Your occupation means your occupation(s) at the time disability began. If you are not employed at that time, your occupation means any occupation you are able to do based on your education, training and experience. *If you are a physician or dentist and have limited your duties to the performance of the usual and customary functions of a specific, professionally recognized medical or dental specialty, we will consider that specialty your occupation.*"

See the difference? Ameritas uses a more specific definition that references physician and dentist duties while Principal's definition is more a blanket, covering a variety of scenarios. We call Ameritas' definition "specialty occupation" while Principal is "own occupation".

In speaking to the back office of a general agent, it was their opinion that the longer legalese is merely a marketing gimmick that allows those companies to charge a higher annual premium.

As I have reviewed over the various carriers, I have found that the carriers who have specialty occupation are charging more than carriers who only have own occupation.

I have never seen any data on claims between the various carriers on disability income, but all of these have had a strong reputation for being direct and relatively easy to deal with.

See the table below for more details on the differences between riders.

	Ameritas	Berkshire/ Guardian	Mass Mutual	MetLife	Principal	Standard
Future Increase Benefit	$10,000	$10,000	$9.000	$11,000	Offered 3 Years after policy starts If declined, Benefit Eliminated	$10,000
True or Specialty Own Occ	Specialty Own Occ	Specialty Own Occ	True Own Occ	Both True & Specialty	True Own Occ	Specialty Own Occ
Income Loss For Residual	15%	15%	20%	20%	20%	20%

For more information, go to www.daviddenniston.com/physicians.
For questions, e-mail: ddenniston@machtig.net
Or call 800-548-1820

| Disability | | | | | | |

3.1 A

3.1 Ac

Another example of the varying legalese between carriers is the difference in the definitions of _residual disability_.

Here, Principal and Ameritas have fairly short definitions while Berkshire, Mass Mutual, Metlife, and Standard have longer definitions.

Here's an example of a shorter definition from Ameritas, "Means due to sickness or injury, your loss of monthly earnings is at least 15% of your prior monthly earnings and you are able to perform one or more, but not all, of the material and substantial duties of your occupation; or you are unable to work in your occupation for 80% or more of the time as was usual prior to the start of your disability."

In comparison, here's the longest definition courtesy of Standard, "During the Initial Period (first 6 months) of partial disability, you are working in your own occupation or any other occupation and due to injury or sickness, you have a loss of duties, or loss of time, or a loss of income and under the regular care of physician. The disability benefit payable each month will equal the basic monthly benefit, regardless of your monthly earnings. After your Initial Period (after 6 months), during the Extended Partial Disability Period, benefits will equal a portion of the basic monthly benefit. If greater than 80% of earnings are lost, 100% of the basic month benefit will be paid."

There's some fascinating differences here.

From our previous table, Ameritas requires at least 15% of prior earnings whereas Standard requires at least 20% of prior earnings.

At first blush, Ameritas looks to have a better benefit because it requires a smaller loss to produce a claim relative to Standard.

However, it gets interesting as you re-read the contract language. When your benefit is turned on from Standard, the first six months of disability will equal the WHOLE monthly benefit. Then, the next six months of disability will be a portion of the basic monthly benefit.

Insurance Guide for Doctors Workbook

In comparison, Ameritas (& most of the other carriers) will only pay a portion of the monthly benefit whether it is sooner or later within the time period of the residual disability.

Lastly, let's focus on the differences between the COLA riders.

There are substantial differences between companies and the discussion is substantive enough to merit dedicating two whole tables to go over the differences.

Ameritas	Berkshire/ Guardian	Mass Mutual
As long as you are receiving a monthly income benefit under this policy, on each anniversary of the onset of disability, we will adjust the monthly income benefit by <u>the lesser of CPI-U or 6%,</u> compounded annually.	While receiving disability benefit payments, Berkshire will adjust your monthly indemnity each year to help keep pace with inflation (<u>3% compounded annually</u>). Prior to age 60, if you are no longer disabled, prior increases to the monthly indemnity will remain on the policy with no extra premium charges until age 67.	After you have been disabled for 12 months your full or partial benefit will be increased at an <u>annually compounded rate of 3%.</u>

AAction St

MetLife	Principal	Standard
This rider may increase your benefits to keep up with inflation. Increases <u>are based on the CPI-U. Increases may not exceed 10%.</u> If there is no change or a decrease in the CPI-U, your adjusted monthly benefit will remain the same.	While you're disabled under the terms of the policy, your benefit is adjusted to help keep up with inflation. <u>A compound interest increase of the lesser of the change in CPI-U up to 3% maximum.</u>	This rider provides for an increase to the monthly benefit payment during a prolonged period of disability based on changes in the CPI-U. The percentage applied is based on the average annual change in the CPI-U up to a 3% maximum.

In s

IIn summary, most of the carriers have up to 3% COLA/CPI adjustment while Ameritas (up to 6%) and MetLife (up to 10%) have better protection from high inflation.

Note that all of these COLA benefits exist AFTER you start a disability benefit, not before it. Your benefit does not adjust upward with inflation which is another reason to consider having a benefit update rider.

This is different than long-term care insurance which has COLA BEFORE and AFTER the long-term care benefit.

Step 3.1: Review over your quotes from Action Steps 2.1 through 2.3. Get the same quotes from another carrier. Record the results in the table below. We did a default of 90 day and 180 day elimination period. Feel free to substitute those for another elimination period, but make sure to compare apples to apples (i.e. 90 day elimination period will be lower priced than 60 day elimination period).

Elimination Period/ Benefit Period	90 Company 1	90 Company 2	180 Company 1	180 Company 2
2 Years				
5 Years				
To Age 65				
To Age 67				
To Age 70				

Action Step 3.2: Review over the tables earlier in this module. How do the carriers you are looking at compare to one another? How do the basic benefits differ? How do the riders differ? Write down your thoughts below

_____
_____
_____
_____.

MODULE Four — Life Insurance Overview. How much to have?

The next important type of insurance for physicians is life insurance.

Are you engaged or married? Do you have any children?

Imagine what it would be like for your family to lose your income. How would it effect their lifestyle? How long could they maintain their lifestyle without your income?

In the last 10 years of being a financial advisor, I have seen unexpected death drastically change the lives and fortunes of my clients. It is an incredibly difficult transition time for families. The last thing you want on top of the emotional distress is financial distress.

As a resident or fellow, <u>if you are single</u> and have little to no obligations, then <u>there is little to no need for external life insurance</u> outside of what is provided at work and you can skim over the rest of the next two modules- educate yourself, but no need to put any of these to action.

However, if you are a resident or fellow and you have a spouse and/or children, I would strongly encourage you to make sure your family is covered!

Like disability insurance, you want to ask yourself, how dependent is my family on my income? Am I a primary breadwinner or a high two-income family?

How much in consumer and house debt do I have?

Note that regardless of the way that you hold life insurance- the proceeds are always income TAX-FREE. The death benefit from a life insurance policy also avoids probate by going directly to your named beneficiaries.

For more information, go to www.daviddenniston.com/physicians.
For questions, e-mail: ddenniston@machtig.net
Or call 800-548-1820

Although I must point out that if your estate is over a certain limit in your state (perhaps as low as $1 million) or over a certain limit federally (above $5 million, rising each year), then you may owe estate taxes. We'll address this later in the text.

There are two basic ways to get life insurance- through work (group term) and by funding it yourself (individual coverage).

Just like disability income insurance, there are pros/cons for having life insurance through work and by funding it yourself.

Although this may seem repetitive due to the similarities with disability income insurance, let me review over the differences between a typical group policy and an individual life insurance policy.

Typical Group Policy	Individual Life Insurance Policy
Little to no medical underwriting required. Neither age or health will usually matter At time of application.	Substantial medical and financial Underwriting required. Better the younger & Healthier you are.
Cheapest Option (usually a minimal amount of Life Insurance is free through employers)	Usually more expensive, depending upon the riders you select
Premiums paid monthly at no extra cost	Premiums best paid annually. Quarterly or Monthly costs more.
Contract terms, premiums, and benefits can Change at any time	Guaranteed term insurance premiums cannot change (but universal life can)
Policy ends when you end employment	Policy is carried by you, before and after employment with any employer

The next most common question is how much should I have? How can I figure it out?

There are several methods to determine how much life insurance one should have.

Insurance Guide for Doctors Workbook

The first method is <u>debt pay-off</u>. The objective here is to eliminate all liabilities and to increase cash flow after a loved one's death. This way your monthly obligations are fairly minimal.

Note that most student loans are NOT included because federally backed loans (i.e. Stafford, Perkins, FFEL) disappear at death. See http://studentaid.ed.gov/repay-loans/forgiveness-cancellation for further details.

I suggest debt pay-off as the minimal amount of life insurance that one should hold.

Also, the debt pay-off method is ideal for a family with both spouses working.

Lastly, I strongly suggest this method for residents and fellows that are looking for affordable insurance, but do not have much of a budget.

This way all liabilities are erased in the event of one spouse's death and you are not over-insured with extra life insurance that you do not need.

The next method is <u>income replacement.</u> The goal with this method is to replace your AFTER-TAX income for a specified time period. I suggest AFTER-TAX because life insurance proceeds are not subject to income taxes.

Also, if you are using your last pay-stub add any current 401k, 403b, or other retirement plan contributions and also add back premiums for medical insurance. This will ensure that you are counting the money that you would have been saving for retirement.

Would you like your family to have 10 years of your income? 20 years? 30 years?

Many folks assume that after 10 years that their spouse has moved on and landed another job, or has another source of income.

Other folks want to protect more and ensure that their family is set for a variety of goals, like paying for college for the kids or that their spouse will never have to work again and will focus on 20 years or 30 years.

A simple rule of thumb is to multiply your current AFTER TAX income times the specified proceeds.

For example, if your pre-tax income is $180,000 and your after-tax income is $140,000, multiply 10 (assuming 10 years is the target) times $140,000 and this gives you total life insurance needed of $1,400,000.

Are you a resident or fellow in your last year (with a spouse and/or kids) before you enter into full-time practice? I strongly suggest starting the underwriting for this amount in the last few months of your residency/fellowship.

The final method is the <u>home sweet home</u> method. Okay, I am being a little (or a lot?) tongue-in-check here, but one could make a case for some folks to add together the debt pay-off method with income replacement.

This way not only are their debts erased, but their income is replaced for a specified time period. I would suggest to use a smaller income replacement time frame- think 5 to 10 years rather than greater than 10 years in order to minimize the cost of insurance.

4.1 Action Step: How much group term insurance do you current have from work?

_____

_____

4.2 Action Step: Calculate the amount of life insurance that you could need based off of the debt pay-off method. How much is (are) your mortgage(s)? Car loan? Credit card debt? Other liabilities? Do NOT include student loans.

_____

_____

_____

_____

4.3 Action Step: Calculate the amount of life insurance that you could need based of the income replacement method. Make sure to use your current AFTER-TAX income and multiply it times the desired time period. If you are not sure, use 10 years, 20 years, and 30 years.

_____

_____

_____

_____

4.4 Action Step: Calculate the amount of life insurance that you could need based of the home-sweet-home method. Make sure to <u>add together</u> the results from Action Step 4.2 and your current AFTER-TAX income and multiply it times the desired time period. Use a smaller time frame of 5 to 10 years to minimize the cost of insurance.

Insurance Guide for Doctors Workbook

_____
_____
_____
_____

MODULE Five | Life Insurance Term vs. Cash Value

Now that we've determined the total amount of life insurance that you need to look into, the next step is to understand the difference between term insurance versus cash value insurance.

I will list several examples and then ask you to get some quotes for your particular situation.

Full disclosure: I have a bias that I need to be intellectually honest about. I consider myself a "term-ite" who is addicted to term life insurance because I am cost averse and like to keep my living expenses low. Yes, I will confess my addiction at the next FPA meeting for insurance agents and financial planners. Anywho, I will address some cases that I feel are appropriate for cash value types of life insurance. It's not always a bad decision.

Differences Between Term and Cash Value Insurance

Guaranteed Term	Whole Life (WL- cash value)	Universal Life (UL- cash value)	Variable Universal Life (VUL- cash value)
Fixed Costs, will not	Fixed costs, will not	Insurance costs can	Insurance costs can

For more information, go to www.daviddenniston.com/physicians.
For questions, e-mail: ddenniston@machtig.net
Or call 800-548-1820

Change for designated Period of time	Change throughout Life of the policy	Vary based off of Interest rates and Actuarial tables	Vary based off of investments and Actuarial tables
Cheapest premium Option	Expensive premiums	Fairly expensive premiums. Depends on how long policy exists.	Fairly expensive premiums. Depends on how long policy exists.
Does not accumulate Cash value	Does accumulate Cash value	Does accumulate Cash value	Does accumulate Cash value
No surrender charges Due to no cash value	Long surrender charges- Must hold policy 10 Years plus to cash out	Long surrender charges- Must hold policy 10 Years plus to cash out	Long surrender charges- Must hold policy 10 Years plus to cash out

In comparison to DI insurance, life insurance rates individuals based on their health. The poorer your health, the more expensive the life insurance will be. This is regardless of the type of life insurance.

The best possible health rating is super preferred followed by preferred plus, then preferred, standard plus, standard, and then tabled ratings.

Tabled ratings is insurance for those with chronic conditions or having some areas that the insurance company would deem to be high risk.

Also, for term insurance, the longer the term, the more expensive it is. The shorter the term, the cheaper it is. You could be extremely cheap and get 10 year term or pay a little bit more and get 20 year term, or pay the most for 30 year term.

Keep in mind that the premiums will increase after the designated period. Work towards having insurance until the time you calculate that you should be close to self-insured or alternatively near retirement.

Insurance Guide for Doctors Workbook

In addition to the differences mentioned between term and cash value insurance, let's walk through some examples so that you can further understand how this could work practically.

I ran some quotes for a 32 year-old for $1,500,000 death benefit of life insurance and entered the results in the tables below.

10 Year Term, Preferred Health	20 Year Term, Preferred Health	30 Year Term, Preferred Health	Universal Life, Preferred Health
$495/ year	$870/ year	$1,380/ year	$3,340

20 Year Term, Preferred Plus Health	20 Year Term, Preferred Health	20 Year Term, Standard Plus Health	20 Year Term, Standard Health
$615/ year	$870/ year	$1,050/ year	$1,350/ year

See how the longer the insurance goes, the more expensive it is? Cash value insurance is the most expensive because it is supposed to last up until you are at least 90 years.

Thus, the 10 year term policy is only about 85% cheaper that the universal life policy!

Also, see how the stronger your health, the cheaper the premium?

Using a 20 year term policy, a preferred plus health rating is 50% cheaper than a standard health rating.

Although I am an admitted "term-ite", there is a time and place for cash value life insurance.

For more information, go to www.daviddenniston.com/physicians.
For questions, e-mail: ddenniston@machtig.net
Or call 800-548-1820

Scenario 1: Let's say that you are maxing out your employer sponsored retirement plan like a 401k or 403b and on top of that you are maxing out your Roth IRA (or back-door Roth IRA).

In addition to that, you have non-retirement money of $100,000 or more which is enough to cover a year or more of living expenses. Also, let's assume you have paid off all of your student loans and high interest rate, non-deductible debt.

This could be a time to consider cash-value life insurance for a portion of your savings. However, keep in mind that the older you get, the more expensive life insurance gets.

Adding more to your non-retirement account or a tax-deferred annuity may be a better fit in this instance if you would like tax deferral and an insurance company guaranteed an income stream down the road.

Scenario 2: A very strong case can be made for using cash value life insurance as a tool for estate tax planning. Using a cash value life insurance policy owned by an irrevocable life insurance trust (ILIT), you can separate out the death benefit of the policy from the rest of the estate.

Why would you want to do this?

Estate taxes! You could potentially save hundreds of thousands of dollars in estate taxes by using an ILIT with a cash value life insurance policy.

For example, the state of Minnesota currently has a $1,000,000 estate tax exemption. This means that they will require the estate to file an estate tax return if any assets in the name of the deceased are over $1,000,000.

This INCLUDES life insurance proceeds, 401k accounts, investment accounts, bank accounts, land, etc.

So, if a person has a $1,000,000 life insurance policy and a $1,500,000 401k- they have a $2,500,000 estate and would get taxed on the remainder over $1,000,000- in this case $1,500,000. In the state of Minnesota, taxes start at 10% and go up. This estate would get hit with an estate tax bill of at least $150,000.

Note that each state has different rules and regulations.

For example, community property states like Texas or Washington divide up the spousal assets equally at the death of the other spouse. Both spouses face the same exact estate issues.

Whereas, Minnesota looks at the assets in each spouse's name and keeps them separate. One spouse could potentially have an estate tax issue while the other does not.

On top of that, there are also federal estate taxes. The exemption in 2013 is $5,250,000. As long as your estate is below that, you don't need to worry about federal estate taxes. However, anything above that has a very steep tax of 40%. Keep in mind that the estate does include life insurance death benefit (unless owned by an ILIT).

I know it's weird! But that's why you need to consult with a financial advisor and/or an attorney if you think you could have this issue.

5.1 Action Step: Get quotes from several companies based on your ideal amount of life insurance to fill in the table below.

10 Year Term, Preferred Health	20 Year Term, Preferred Health	30 Year Term, Preferred Health	Universal Life, Preferred Health
10 Year Term, Standard Health	20 Year Term, Standard Health	30 Year Term, Standard Health	Universal Life, Standard Health

5.2 Action Step: Re-visit scenario 1 and 2 to see if it may make sense to look at a cash value life insurance policy. For example, calculate the current amount of your estate. Is it worth looking into a cash value irrevocable life insurance policy?

_____

_____

_____

MODULE Six | What Do I Spend Monthly & Where Can I Improve?

The final step in our journey is to discover and strategize how much you can save without substantially changing your lifestyle. This can be very time intensive if you want to understand every nut and bolt on a weekly basis. However, it can also be pretty straight-forward and easy to do if you want to look only on a monthly or bi-monthly basis.

6.1 Action step: Buy or sign up for a cash flow/spending tracking software programs. Common examples include Mint.com, Quicken, MVelopes, and countless others. We use EMoney Advisor. For any resident or fellow, we provide this software for free. For a quick overview of this program, check out:

http://www.emoneyadvisor.com/emacorp/video.aspx?vid=box&w=853&h=480&lang=en

Some are free and other cost money. Some banks and credit cards offer some software as well. Explore one or two of these programs.

Choose one and sign up for it.

6.2 Action step: Link in all of your assets and liabilities through the service you selected. This typically involves log-ins through the financial sources that you use.

6.3 Action step: The best programs will automatically categorize your expenses. It may not be entirely correct.

Consider looking through the activity or correcting the categories.

Common examples that usually need categorizing include checks that are written, mom & pop stores, and small restaurants.

6.4 Action step: In the software, Go to the section that puts your monthly spending all together. For example, in E-Money Advisor, the 'Trends' tab. Fill in the charts below...

My Monthly Spending:

This Month	Previous Month	Two Months Ago	Three Months Ago

My Biggest 4 Expense Categories

This Month	Previous Month	Two Months Ago	Three Months Ago
1.	1.	1.	1.
2.	2.	2.	2.
3.	3.	3.	3.
4.	4.	4.	4.

For more information, go to www.daviddenniston.com/physicians.
For questions, e-mail: ddenniston@machtig.net
Or call 800-548-1820

6.5 Action step: As you look at the data above, find two of three ways that you can lower your monthly expense. Perhaps, consider shopping for lower cost medical/auto/home insurance. See if you can refinance your mortgage. Cut out a trip to Starbucks, eat out less often, take lunch to work more often, etc, etc. Write them down below:

_____

_____

_____

6.6 Action step: Now that we've talked about expenses. The next logical step is to think about ways to increase your income. If you've increased your income and decreased your expenses, you are well on your way on the path to financial prosperity!

How have you increased your income in the past? How can you increase your income in the future?

_____

_____

_____

What training or additional education or certification may allow you to gain a promotion at work or more desirable to other employers or clients?

_____

_____

_____

_____

Consider starting your own small business or moonlighting. Many people today sell trinkets or hobbies through E-Bay or Amazon.com. What are your talents? What are your passions?

Alternatively, check out Nineline.com for moonlighting opportunities for physicians. You can get paid $150/hour or more. One of my physician friends is now making more money from moonlighting than from his full-time job. What opportunities could be available to you?

_____

_____

_____

Final Thoughts

Congratulations! You've just accomplished something that very few people have every done in their lives.

You have taken the time to invest into your future. You have explored disability income insurance and life insurance. You've learned about the most important features to add onto these policies and how to minimize cost.

Just as importantly, you've also set up some tools to help monitor spending as well as to increase your income.

Take the next step- implement those promises you made to yourself.

We cannot control so many things in our lives- the weather, your favorite sports team winning the big game, being sick, a family member passing away, children that make poor decisions, and so much more.

However, your insurance policies and how you treat them **are in your power**. Take control today. Live within your means. You can do it!

I encourage you to revisit this workbook on an annual basis. I will make updates based on your feedback. So, please let me know your experience and where I can improve.

If you would like any additional support and to learn more about how I can serve you, please feel free to contact me anytime at ddenniston@machtig.net or call me at (800) 548-1890.

Let's take this journey together and get you on the path to financial freedom.

Warm Regards,

Dave Denniston

www.ingramcontent.com/pod-product-compliance
Lightning Source LLC
Chambersburg PA
CBHW081801170526
45167CB00008B/3284